# The Smart & Easy Guide To Personal Finance & Family Budgeting: Your Financial Workbook to Budget Management, Saving Money Programs, Paying Off Debt & Planning for the Future

Richard Norris

# Legal Stuff

## Copyright Information

Copyright © 2013 Eric Welke. All rights reserved worldwide.

No part of this publication may be replicated, redistributed, or given away in any form without the prior written consent of the author and publisher.

Checkmate Marketing Group LLC

## Earnings Disclaimer

EVERY EFFORT HAS BEEN MADE TO ACCURATELY REPRESENT THIS PRODUCT AND IT'S POTENTIAL. IN TERMS OF EARNINGS, THERE IS NO GUARANTEE THAT YOU WILL EARN ANY MONEY USING THE TECHNIQUES AND IDEAS IN THIS MATERIAL. INFORMATION PRESENTED ON THIS BOOK IS NOT TO BE INTERPRETED AS A PROMISE OR GUARANTEE OF EARNINGS. EARNING POTENTIAL IS ENTIRELY DEPENDENT ON THE PERSON USING OUR PRODUCT, IDEAS AND TECHNIQUES.

ANY CLAIMS MADE OF ACTUAL EARNINGS OR EXAMPLES OF ACTUAL RESULTS CAN BE VERIFIED UPON REQUEST. YOUR LEVEL OF SUCCESS IN ATTAINING THE RESULTS CLAIMED IN OUR MATERIALS DEPENDS ON THE TIME YOU DEVOTE TO THE PROGRAM, IDEAS AND TECHNIQUES MENTIONED, YOUR FINANCES, KNOWLEDGE AND VARIOUS SKILLS. SINCE THESE FACTORS DIFFER ACCORDING TO INDIVIDUALS, WE CANNOT GUARANTEE YOUR SUCCESS OR INCOME LEVEL.

ANY AND ALL FORWARD LOOKING STATEMENTS HERE OR ON ANY OF OUR SALES MATERIAL ARE INTENDED TO EXPRESS OUR OPINION OF EARNINGS POTENTIAL. MANY FACTORS WILL BE IMPORTANT IN DETERMINING YOUR ACTUAL RESULTS AND NO GUARANTEES ARE MADE THAT YOU WILL ACHIEVE RESULTS SIMILAR TO OURS OR ANYONE ELSES. NO GUARANTEES ARE MADE THAT YOU WILL ACHIEVE ANY RESULTS FROM OUR IDEAS AND TECHNIQUES IN OUR MATERIAL.

## Limitation of Liability

THE MATERIALS IN THIS BOOK ARE PROVIDED "AS IS" WITHOUT ANY EXPRESS OR IMPLIED WARRANTY OF ANY KIND INCLUDING WARRANTIES OF MERCHANTABILITY, NONINFRINGEMENT OF INTELLECTUAL PROPERTY, OR FITNESS FOR ANY PARTICULAR PURPOSE. IN NO EVENT SHALL OR ITS AGENTS OR OFFICERS BE LIABLE FOR ANY DAMAGES WHATSOEVER (INCLUDING, WITHOUT LIMITATION, DAMAGES FOR LOSS OF PROFITS, BUSINESS INTERRUPTION, LOSS OF INFORMATION, INJURY OR DEATH) ARISING OUT OF THE USE OF OR INABILITY TO USE THE MATERIALS, EVEN IF HAS BEEN ADVISED OF THE POSSIBILITY OF SUCH LOSS OR DAMAGES.

## Table of Contents

Introduction ........................................................................... 6
What Is Your Current Financial Status? ............................ 12
How to Budget ...................................................................... 18
Avoid the Pitfalls - 3 Reasons for Budget Failure ........... 21
What Makes A Good Budget? ............................................. 23
The Family Budget Process ................................................ 24
Points to Remember ............................................................ 29
Bills, Bills, Bills ..................................................................... 32
Help in a Crisis ..................................................................... 35
Living with a Budget ........................................................... 37
Accepting the Negative and Positive Changes ................ 38
The Dreaded 'D' Word: Debt .............................................. 39
Family Budgeting and Children ......................................... 44
… And Finally ....................................................................... 46
We Want Your Feedback on This Book! ........................... 47

# Introduction

The above quote seems to reflect today's general nature of family budgeting. But in this piece, however, we shall try to take a more positive view. We shall approach budgeting as a financial management tool, making sure that it is focused on being easy to use.

When you inquire why more families do not make budgets you find out pretty quickly that there is a great deal of doubt about whether a budget is really needed or not.

Unfortunately, in depth research has shown that many families are trapped in the "What comes in must go out" cycle.

Perhaps many families believe that budgeting is an unnecessary chore which makes them face the financial situation is a depressing and burdening way. They may have the idea that if they do not talk about their finances, that they do not have to think about it. Basically, they put it out of their mind in order to avoid the stress that money undoubtedly causes in the majority of people.

Perhaps others think they are locked in a spiral of Spend, Spend, Spend, and no matter how hard they try to get out of debt, it just never seems to stop. We need to think about these questions. How can we stop these vicious cycles? How can we change people's mind set about family finance? What can be done in order to encourage families to make a budget and stick to it?

"How to set up a Family Budget" will focus on the ways to set up sound, realistic budgets. We will show you how to stick by them, learn from failure, and celebrate the successes. Overall it is a way of empowerment and a way for families to see the reasons why they should have a family budget.

Eventually there will be money spare at the end of the month. Savings will grow and debt will eventually be consolidated. Families will be able to build their wealth. By becoming more aware of their financial responsibilities they are, by default, having more control of their lives. This is when critical thought patterns and spending habits are changed.

Budgeting is seen as an accurate measurement of success when significant behavioral transformation is taking place on the landscape of the family budget, spending habits and financial patterns we observe over time!

Ask yourself this; do you struggle to make your money last the whole month? Does it feel like you never make any inroads into clearing your credit card debt?

Here's a little reminder; when money has been spent, it is gone for good. But are you worried that you need to save for your retirement? Or for a nice nest egg? Then in this book you can find advice on how to create a family budget, how to implement and stick by it, and how to revise it as times change.

Budgeting is a dynamic process. It should be flexible enough to be able to accommodate changes in resources and it should reflect your financial circumstances and needs.

It is not about what you cannot afford, but about how to use your money wisely. Whether this be in invest or spending the dollars you have earned. It is about making your money go further.

The purpose of this guide is to assist you with developing your own personal and household budget, to change your spending habits, and learn just how to deal with financial problems that may occur from time to time.

We will look at ways to save money. But more than that we'll look at what needs to change in order to become more disciplined and better with money. We will see if you need to re-evaluate your behaviour and attitudes to money.

For example, being a bargain hunter looking for good buys, cutting down on careless spending, being on the lookout for careless credit card spending and letting the person who handles money best in your household actually take care of it, are all good examples of what we mean when it comes to doing the best for your financial welfare.

In the simplest terms, a budget is a spending plan. It shows your incomings and your outgoings. A spending plan can help to see where you money is going and helps you be prepared for paying bills. It can eliminate the stress of money since you know where it is going at all times, and just what you have to work with. For many people the uncertainty they feel with their finances is eliminated once they make a budget.

It is simply a matter of making a plan that you can live within and adhere to. But it is a task which a lot of people dread, or believe that it is more complex than it actually is. Due to this, many people never make a budget and they do end up spending their lives living from paycheck to paycheck, unprepared for any emergency that may arise and having no savings to rely on for anything.

The guide will help to dispel these fears and show you how easy it is to set up a budget that is systematic, efficient and straightforward.

There are lots of reasons why we choose to spend money. It may be through necessity, or as an indulgence. Some people may spend a lot of money on clothes, and some may have to have an annual vacation. Other people spend money due to their emotional state, as this is a form of therapy for them.

But whether you are making financial decisions for yourself or for the household you may have to make adjustments based on your financial freedom.

Through this guide we will help you to answer those important questions when setting up a budget for the household, and allow you to start thinking about your financial future.

First of all you need to realize that budgeting is not only about reining in spending. It is also about learning to make well informed decisions and the act of living on a budget.

We will be focusing on the practical application of systematic budgeting, and look at some 'best practice' suggestions. By the end, you should feel more confident and empowered to create a suitable financial plan for your family budget.

Let's take the first step.

Assess where you and your family are financially at the moment. This will involve looking at what money you have coming into the family and what is going out.

- Were you able to do so? If no, why not? What is lacking?

- Did you have all the data and information? This includes having all your credit card statements and other bills that you get each month.

- Do you have disposable income?

Households have varying circumstances and needs and so each of us will deal with our finances differently. But there are certain criteria that we all need to address. The aim of setting up a budget is to help you discern:

- If you need to cut costs

- If you need to gain control of your spending

- If you need to start saving, which is something that most people need to start doing

- When you will be able to build wealth and assets.

Let's now look further into the value and advantages of having a budget.

Many families live by a simplistic rule; money is earned and then spent. This is usually driven by the daily needs and wants. There is no plan at all. There is a cycle of spending whatever comes in and not thinking about what could happen in the future.

Unfortunately, many families have fallen into a vicious circle of debt, as spending increases while wages and income does not. This is why you need to be aware of your finances and at least monitor your out comings. No one wants to find themselves in a situation in which they have to borrow money in order to cover a bill that they should be able to pay with their income.

With this being said, looking at what you earn and how you spend this is the best place to start with making a budget. As this is the fundamental information that is going to be required to even begin the process of knowing what you have in terms of money, and what is being paid out.

Think about your financial situation, do you truly know where you stand? Many of us tend to underplay how much spend. People are shocked when they actually sit down to assess their position. For example, many people are surprised to learn that they spend more on entertainment every month than they spend on fuel for their cars. You need to consider a) your financial worth, b) your financial goals, and c) the time you want to take to achieve your goals.

Start by gathering together all the relevant information that you will need. Bank statements, wage slips, tax returns, recent credit reports, and financial assets statements. You cannot get where you want to be without knowing where you currently are. Your budget will serve you as a road map towards your financial targets.

Let us now look at the questions surrounding family budgeting. These are the dynamic processes that form the elements of "family budgeting". For this you need to be asking…

**WHAT?**

# What Is Your Current Financial Status?

Anything that you have of value goes into defining your financial worth. All of your assets are part of your financial picture. Money is checking accounts, bank accounts, saving accounts. Money from investments portfolios, stocks, pensions, etc.

Firstly, consider your wages. How much is your salary after deductions? Remember to take into consideration when you get paid; weekly, monthly, fortnightly. Set your budget around the time scale of your wages, i.e. if you get paid monthly, your budget should this. For many people who have a fluctuating income, this can be harder, but this is a step that cannot be skipped. However, you need to assess why your budget fluctuates. For example, those who get paid overtime may count on this from time to time, however, this overtime pay should not be included since it may not be regular pay. Only your regular salary needs to be included in this equation.

Do you have any other sources of income? They could be bonuses or seasonal pay. If they are not regular, it may be wise to leave them out of the budget and focus on what you can rely on coming in regularly, just as if this were overtime pay that you may get throughout the year.

Have you considered everything? Everything that can be turned into cash needs to be included; all your bank accounts, savings, loans, credit union accounts, money market accounts, certificates of deposit, even Christmas Saving club accounts!

If you have a lot of accounts and money spread out over them, it may be an idea to consolidate them. This can save on bank fees and make it easier to track money. If you have a handle on what is coming in and out of accounts it is also easier to see if there are any suspicious transaction. Plus, it makes knowing just how much money you have much easier than having to figure out three different accounts.

Many people find it a revelation just to do this simple task which is to form the basis for deeper analysis of your finances. There are those who do not realize that they have so little coming in and much more going out, or even those who realize they have more coming in than what they thought.

Most of us are used to having short-term financial goals when it comes to budgeting. We need to change our mind-set to looking at longer term planning. If you are able to change your mind set, getting your budget to work for you is going to be much easier.

Don't stop setting short term goals, but combining them with mid to long term goals is the baseline for you future financial planning and form part of a definite structured plan. It will help you to focus on your needs, but install form some financial discipline. Think of the formula of using short term and mid term goals in order to reach the long term goal. For example, your long term goal may be to pay off all your debt and start putting money into savings. The short term goal may be to pay off your lowest balanced credit card. Once you do this, you keep adding in short term goals, with a mid term goal of putting $50 into savings each month. Before long, you have built to the long term goal.

Many family budgeting guides will focus on one area of financial planning. Some will suggest frugal living and focus on shaving costs. Some will focus on becoming debt free, and how to choose the best forms of credit. In this guide we will do things a little different. It is hands-on with a practical approach to making the right financial choices. The aim is to set up a solid budget for your household.

**WHO?**

Every family is different with their own different situations to deal with. That is why there is no 'cookie-cutter' solution for all. If there were a simple solution that applied to every family out there, there would really be no reason why people dread starting a budget. And this is why we have to take a hands on approach so that you can learn what will suit you best and not all of the tips we are about to look at will be applicable to your situation.

The information that we will look at should be evaluated in the context of your own position. I.E. Work out whether this will work for you. Remember that, if in doubt, contact a financial adviser who can work out whether a decision will be right for your financial health. In many situations it is the best practice to gather as much information as possible, to access all the help that is available to you.

Because there are so many different types of family this guide has tried to offer something for most people. So if you are a nuclear family, single parent, mixed marriage family, or whether you have double income, one income, or income from welfare, we hope that there is something for you to take away from this and apply this towards your own budget in order to get your family started on the right path towards financial freedom.

## WHY?

Family budgeting is a structured activity of dealing with your resources and your obligations. You need to understand the reality of your situation. One way to do so is to put all of your spending obligations into categories. This will show you, firstly, how much you are spending, and, secondly, where you could be potentially wasting money.

So, for example, take 4 headlines, Necessities, Family Allowances, Personal Allowances, Pocket Expenses. Now put everything that you spend money on under the correct heading, and how much. Be honest, otherwise there is no point. If you are unsure of the amount, it is almost best to estimate high rather than low, since it could give you a pleasant surprise at the end of the month when you have more money left than what you would have thought. Here's a more detailed example,

- Necessities; Groceries $X, Rent/Mortgage $X, Utilities $X, Car upkeep $X, Insurance $X, Pet Upkeep $X, School Lunches $X, Tax $X, Savings $X, College Fund $X ETC

- Family Allowances; Days Out $X, Home Improvement $X, Christmas $X, Birthdays $X, Furniture $X, Vacation $X ETC

- Personal Allowances; Clothing $X, Recreation (books, cd's, DVDs,) $X, Hair Cut $X, Nights Out $X, Donations $X, Hobbies $X, ETC

- Pocket Expenses; Lunch at work $X, Candy $X, Parking $X, Newspapers $X, Mail $X, Drinks $X ETC

Put the total at the end of each category. You may have not realized that you spent so much on clothing, for example, and so now you have found a way to cut back.

People budget for all kinds of reasons;

- To gain control of their financial lives

- To gain control of their monthly spending

- To be better prepared should the worse happen

- To save for major purchases

- To leave their children a nest egg

- To save for their children's' college fees

- To get out of debt

- To expand their lifestyle

- To possible retire early

- To eliminate money as a source of stress

- To become more self reliant

## WHEN? AND WHERE?

We can combine these two questions together with one simple statement.

When is the best to start a budget? **NOW**. And where is the best time to start? **HERE**. Assuming that you're reading this at home of course!

This is an issue that demands attention. So don't postpone it. You need to work out what is going wrong if you are financial difficulties. The sooner that you learn the need for a budget is a necessity, the better off you are going to be. Those who adapt to a new budget are often surprised at just how much stress this relieves from their daily life.

**HOW?**

# How to Budget

Let's think about how we think about money and our relationship with it. This involves looking at how you view money. Do you view this as something that is meant to be spent? Do you believe in saving for a rainy day? Also think about how you view credit cards, are these just a way for you to get what you want and pay for this later? With these types of questions, your view about money in general is going to help you determine just how you should budget, as in what types of goals you should be striving for.

Firstly, if you focus on the short term spending, then shift this to thinking about savings, planning ahead and financial success. It is also critical to know much income you have, as discussed above. Those who think on the short term basis often look at their money as coming in and going out. These types of people may often save for something that they want, then spend the money, never thinking twice about planning for the future. These are people who live in the here and now. Realistically, there are more people who believe in short term spending versus long term planning.

Next, think about how you are possible enticed into spending. For instance, adverts, retail psychology or from a need to "Keep up with the Jones's." None of these are reasons for spending. You can quickly create a false sense of wealth from over spending on unnecessary luxuries that you feel you NEED to have. It is easy for someone to fall into this line of thinking. The consumer market is huge and it is this way because people believe that they need to have those things in order to survive. For example, having the latest car even though their old car was fine. It is this type of thinking that can get a person into debt in a very fast time period.

Those who think like this are simply increasing their debt and pushing their money resources to the limit. In order to combat this, a person should always ask yourself, 'Do I need this?' if you answer 'no', then ask 'Then why am I buying it?' If you are still set on buying then ask 'Can I afford this?' If the answer is 'no', then re-ask 'Why am I buying it?' If you can afford it, ask yourself 'Could this money be better spent?' Constantly question what you are buying and why. This is the best way to get a handle on over spending. In worse case scenarios, if you cannot think of a reason why you should not buy something, consider leaving it and thinking about it for a few days. In a few days if this is still something you need, then reexamine your budget to see if you can afford this with your cash, rather than putting this on credit. The majority of those who wait for a purchase are often able to see the purchase as being one that they really do not need.

Next, set some aims and goals. Make sure that they are realistic. Some examples could be:

- No cash advances as these types of advances can charge double the interest as the interest rate that the credit card is charging. In addition, they are always the last thing that are paid off on a credit card.

- Not using credit cards to make ends meet as this is just putting a person in a constant revolving circle of debt. Instead, the person should allot for how much they can afford with their income and this is all.

- Start saving a certain amount of money each month. This is a great goal even if all you can afford to put away each month is $20. Overtime, this will compile and give you a good little savings account.

- Pay more money on your debt. Even those who make an extra $30 on their payments each month are paying on the principle of the debt, which in turns lowers the balance much faster.

- Making no purchases on credit which is the only way that the person is going to see that their debt is lowering.

- Have a set amount of cash each week that can be used on expenses such as eating out or the like, this type of goal can really help a person to get a good handle on their spending.

You can tailor your own goals to suit your situation. Don't forgot to give yourself a little reward from time to time to celebrate your success. But keep in mind that it is only one small success in the grand scheme of things. So don't go overboard. You reward can be something as simple as getting ice cream after work, or treating yourself to a movie. It is best to make this reward something that you have cut yourself off from in order to encourage yourself to continue with your budget.

There is a lot of free financial software available online to help you come up with a detailed family budget and to manage your finances. This software can help to keep track of expenses and income, while providing a tangible way to see what you are spending. Also, there are free money saving email newsletters that offer tips, advice and other financial information that you can routinely put into your life to help your budget.

# Avoid the Pitfalls - 3 Reasons for Budget Failure

Despite best efforts, many people become discouraged with the activity of budgeting. This is to be expected, as budgeting is something that gets better with time. Those who do get discouraged are often left believing that the budget is not helpful, since they are not seeing any rewards from this. There are three main reasons why a person fails at their budget, it is best to know what this is in order to combat this in your own budget:

1) Negative Attitude

   A positive mental attitude improves chances of success 100%. Continual viewing everything with negativity increases you chances of becoming disillusioned. Keep your desired goal end in mind and keep reminding yourself why you are doing this.

2) Lack of Motivation

   Securing financial security, getting debt free, or saving can be long processes. If you are doing this for the wrong reasons, you will quickly come unstuck. As I said above, keep reminding yourself why you're doing this. Reward yourself for the success. Learn from the failures, and move on. You will find that if you include your entire family, that they can help to motivate you to continue with your budget, and you can motivate them to keep on with the set budget.

3) Unrealistic Expectations

   Keep your feet on the floor. Just because you expect to free up some cash by curbing spending, does not mean you will be a millionaire. Did you expect changes to be significant in a short space of time? Realize that it can be a long slog, with little or no changes noticeable for a while. Don't expect miracles to happen overnight when it comes to your finances and it may take months before you really start to see a difference in what you are doing.

Budgeting is like a marathon, rather than a sprint. It is about endurance and discipline. There are going to be times in which you may not be able to stick to your budget, and this is fine. Emergencies and unexpected circumstances pop up from time to time, but it is important that you try to stick to the budget as best as you can.

# What Makes A Good Budget?

Again, the factors that go into making a good budget depend largely on you situation. There are some criteria which will be universal, but ultimately, a good budget is one that helps your financial situation. The following factors may be some of the more important ones.

- It is realistic to the person's situation

- Is factual

- Is accurate, which does mean looking at the budget periodically

- It is mutually agreed on by the entire family, as this budget affects the entire family so everyone should have input

- Involves communication

- It is collaborative with the main head of house and those who contribute to the income

- Set in the present

- Future orientated

- Enlightens financial past to show just what you need to change for the future

Without a good budget in place, you cannot expect for this budget to work. With this being said, you need to make sure that you make your budget and include everyone in order to make this work.

# The Family Budget Process

So, by now you have looked at your incomings and outgoings, and you have sorted your priorities and come up with some necessary financial obligations. By now you should be at the stage where you can balance your budget. In other words, make sure your incoming money covers what you pay out. You may already have a sense of this from the previous exercises. Income – Outcome = $? Balance.

Let's quickly recap:

A) You should know how much money you have to spend each month.

B) You should know on what you generally spend your money on.

C) You should know how much you spend each month.

D) You should know your balance at the end of each month.


So, are your expenses covered by your earnings? Yes- a positive result! But don't get too complacent and start increasing your spending. Don't forget that prices will invariably rise, but your income may not. It would perhaps be better to save the extra as a kind of fund against unexpected costs. Or, you could try to pay off some of your debts a little quicker. If not, then it is time to look at what can be cut from your budget.

However, take a look back at your spending. Have you found anything that you could cut back on? Where you shocked by the amount you spent on something insignificant? For example, did you notice you spend hundreds of dollars a month on entertainment, and this is something that you rarely get to enjoy? If so, this could be one area that you could cut down to save a bit more money each month. Getting into a habit of checking your spending could be a good idea in the long term, should anything unexpected happen to your situation.

In order to start cutting costs, you have to take a few steps in order to complete this. For those who notice their incoming funds are not covering their outgoing funds, then they first need to look back over you're the list of what you spend money on and decide what needs to go. This, I'm afraid, is entirely at your discretion. There are no hard and fast rules that will fit everyone. One piece of advice is that you keep calm and keep being realistic. Don't make cuts with things you cannot be without- rent/mortgage, utilities, etc. Keep in mind, that is may be a bit difficult to make these cuts and stick to them for a while. You have gotten used to a certain type of living, and making do without something can be a hard process to get used to.

Have a look at what you spend on luxuries. Making little cuts here and there is a good place to start. Cancel your newspaper subscription, stop buying candy and sodas, cut back on socializing, start taking your lunch from home to work, rather than going out to eat, and the like. It is things like this that may seem small but overtime they will save you a great deal of money. You could downgrade your cable subscription. Maybe not take a vacation this year. Agree to not go over board at Christmas. Buy cheaper grocery brands, or use thrift stores. Maybe even take up couponing for the groceries you need and utilizing the sales that your local grocery stores are having. All of this cutting will add up over time.

Keep going over your budget, noting how much you have cut. Also, it may be very useful to actually make real time notes every time you spend money so that you can see if there are any other expenses that you did not originally take into consideration. This will act as a kind of 'financial diary', keeping track of you spending patterns. Note every bill you pay, and every time you withdraw cash at an ATM. It may even be helpful to note what you are spending your cash on as this can give you a better idea of just where your money is going.

Things will eventually change by your efforts or ones you have no control over. This is a key reason why you should keep going back and go through the budgeting process regularly; so that you are always aware of your financial situation. As you should have realized by now, it does no good to stick your head in the sand. Remember, not all changes are bad, but you always need to be aware of them.

It has become the nature of society today to live in the moment. We are endlessly encouraged to spend, to enjoy life now. The commercials on TV are designed to make you think you need XYZ product, rather than it being an extravagance. Try to minimize contact with these adverts. If you constantly receive advertising emails from companies that you have used in the past, then unsubscribe from their email list. Turn the sound off on the TV when the adverts come on. Bin or recycle the 'extras' you get in newspapers that are adverts. Always remember that those infomercials you see are targeted for one purpose and this is to get you to buy a product or service.

As we have seen in the previous pages, the process of starting to create your family budget is not a difficult one. It just requires honesty and dedication to make it work.

By continual revising and updating your budget you are better equipped to deal with any changes in circumstances.

There is no getting away from the fact that money is necessity in our lives and will remain ever present. There is no escape from this fact. And this is true across the whole world. There are different currencies, financial structures, procedures or financial philosophies but it is present everywhere in some format.

Sometimes it is hard to feel that you are at the mercy of the wheels of the global economy, and the government's response to money matters. We hear on the news daily stories of banking rules, monetary regulations, trading principles, financial ethics or scare stories of economic meltdown. Consequentially, our own family budget seems overwhelmingly insignificant. This is not the case.

Good money management skills are crucial for your own survival in a difficult world. Additionally, your children should pick up on your handling of money and learn the basics in money management from you. This is why it is an important responsibility to get a handle on sound budgeting.

You need to give your children the best start by setting a good example. It is likely that if they see irresponsibility spending as the norm, then they will continue this pattern. They are likely to also end up being trapped in the vicious downward spiral of easy but expensive credit and with a money-in-money-out mentality.

As parents you have an opportunity to teach your children solid financial skills from an early age. They will be equipped with these skills for life, and will hopefully be able to use them when they eventually have to make family budgets of their own.

## Points to Remember

Looking back over what we have already discussed here are some points that will give you additional guidance when making a budget.

1) Face the Facts- Assess your worth, and home and financial situation honestly and keeping in mind your main purpose.

2) Be Thorough and Critical- Take a factual look at your fiscal situation. Use unbiased information, such as a credit report, tax return etc. If you need to, use a professional to help you. An accountant, broker, or financial adviser should be able to help.

3) Plan a Road Map- Formulate some financial goals and lay out a step by step plan of how to get there.

4) Commit- Commit the necessary time and effort. Don't underestimate how much time it will take. Make it a top priority in your household chores.

5) Definition- Reflect on how you came up with your sense of financial worth. Is it based on facts, or misguided beliefs.

6) Up to date- Make sure you keep going over your budget, making any additional changes. Time frame wise, most people find that looking over their budget monthly at the beginning and every few months afterward is enough to ensure they are not missing anything and they do see some results of their financial planning.

7) The Real Cost- When you purchase something on credit, do you know what the real cost will be? This means thinking about how much interest is going to be charged.

8) Go for Goal- Financial goals are way of giving yourself something to focus on in the short or long term. When you complete your goal, you get a psychological boost. Be sure to make short, mid term and long term goals so that you are consistently getting rewarded for your efforts, as this will make budgeting much easier.

9) Increase Your Knowledge- Try to learn about finances and economics. This will help you to understand reports that you hear on the news, and also make you more familiar with the financial language is you ever wanted to make investments etc.

10) Avoid Expensive Friends- Be honest with your friends that you are on a tight budget. You will quickly see those who respect that, and those who don't. Some people may constantly try to persuade you to go on nights out, or for fancy meals- these are the people to avoid. They know your situation but have made no effort to take it into consideration.

11) Good Habits- Sticking to a budget is also about getting into good habits. There are hundreds of little ways to save money, here are a few tips to get you started.

- Learning not to buy on impulse which will take time to learn as it has become a habit that is not easy to break

- Searching for the best deals whether this be on groceries or clothing. There is no reason to pay full price when in the next week it may be on sale.

- Using credit cards only in emergencies and only when you do not have the saved funds to cover the emergency.

- Not using short term/ pay day loans as these require paying back a huge amount of interest.

- Buy generics/ cheaper brands as these can be up to forty percent less than the popular brand.

- Turn the thermostat down, just by turning your thermostat down a few degrees in the winter and up a few degrees in the summer can save you hundreds per year on your utility bills.

- Save energy and make your home energy efficient

- Shop around and get quotes for insurance or energy companies, as taking a few hours to do this can save you hundreds during a given year.

- Cut back on cell phone use and consider lowering your monthly plan to save money.

- Use a dental school for treatment- massive discount if you trust the trainee dentists to do your teeth.

12) Make Notes- If you cannot account for all your spending, then makes notes of what you spend. Carry a notepad with you and write down everything from a packet of gum to a tank of gas.

13) Work Together- Get all the family involved in the budgeting process. Ask for their ideas and input to try and make things work. They could have some great ideas which you would have never thought of. It also means that they will be more likely to appreciate the need for a budget and, therefore, stick to it.

This booklet is not going to be the definitive source of information on family budgeting. There are lots of good ways to learn more about finances and budgeting. You only have to search online, and you will find a wealth of free information. Your local library may have books that you can borrow, or there may be adult education classes that you can take.

But don't forget to ask other members of your family. The older generations in your family may have lots of practical 'Make Do and Mend' suggests that they had to live by in harder times.

# Bills, Bills, Bills

Let's take a little look at the universally disliked activity of paying your bills. Hopefully the previous tasks have helped you know what bills you have and how much they come to. There's no getting around the fact that you will have to pay them, so here are a few ideas to make this process as easy and painless as possible.

1. The first thing to do is make a list of the bills, how much and when they are due. You can use the information you gathered in the other exercises to help you. Organize them into chronological order i.e. in the order of when they need to be paid. I would organize them like this, instead of amount because you will be able to determine when your income comes in relation to when the bills are due.

2. For example, let's say you get paid $1,000 on the first of each month, but the biggest bill, your rent of $500, comes out on the $25^{th}$. This means that you have to make sure that you don't spend that money. But life does not't always run that smoothly, and 25 days is a long time to hold onto that amount of money. At least writing down when bills are due you are more aware of your obligations.

3. Mark when the bills are due on each month of a calendar. Also make sure you note how they are paid- by cash/ check, Direct Debit/ Standing order, by card etc. You will be reminded constantly when bills are due.

4. There are a number of techniques to avoid spending money that needs to be kept for bills. Not all of these may apply to you, but there should be something here which is helpful to your particular situation.

- Open a Household Account- It may be worth opening up a new checking account where you can deposit money for bills, and from which all bills are paid. This is very useful if you get paid monthly.

  One thing to ensure is that you never set up an Overdraft facility on this account. You will only end up in more debt as this allows you to take out more money than you have, yet the penalities for doing so are going to be anywhere from $25 to $50 for every occurrence the person has.

- If you are paid weekly, then you need to make sure that the large bills are covered. If you work out your total monthly bills and then work out how much each week should be deposited into the Household account to cover everything.

    However, if you are going to start this method, then you need to be aware of when bills are due. I.E. What happens if the largest bill amount is due on the first week of the month? Straight away you do not have enough to cover the first week's bills. The answer to this is to make sure that you choose which week of the month on which to start depositing money. This will ensure that you will have saved up enough to cover everything. Don't be tempted to use credit cards to cover it as this can mean more money going out each month due to high interest rates.

- The 1-2-3-4 plan- Start off similar to above, but start with the premise of a 4 week month. Now, we know that months differ in the amount of days each one has- January has 31, February has 28/9, April has 30. So, if you get paid on a Friday and you deposit your set amount then. When there is a $5^{th}$ Friday in a month, you get an extra pay packet.

    This does mean, however, that each weekly amount will be more than if you used the previous technique. And again, make sure you are covered for all bills. Try to use the extra pay packet constructively, save it, invest it or use it to pay off debt.

There is one important thing to consider when talking about bills; not all bills come in monthly or weekly. Some bills are quarterly, half yearly or annually. Again, making a separate list of these is the first step. These bills could be things like tax bill, car registration, insurance etc. You could also include events like Christmas or Birthdays, so that you at least have something put aside for these. Again, there are a number of ways to tackle these one off payments. You could divide their total by 12 and put enough away each month. You could also see if it's possible to spread the payments of 12 months, and turn one big bill into 12 smaller ones (don't forget the possibility of having to pay interest). In the end, it is about find a way that is manageable for you.

# Help in a Crisis

We have all been in some kind of trouble at some point in our lives. An unforeseen event occurs and it causes a crisis. It is a natural reaction to panic or to over react, or even to try to ignore it completely. None of these reacts will solve the problem however. You need to take a practical view and work out what can be done. This is not always as easy as it sounds. It can be a very trying period in your life- but it is at these times when we learn Life's lessons best.

Admitting there's a problem is the very first step. It is like at AA meetings you need to be able to say "My name is Bob, and I'm an alcoholic". You have to be able to admit it to yourself and to outsiders before help can begin. Financial affairs have always been considered a bit 'taboo', something you don't talk about to people. But sitting down with a close friend of relative and telling them your problems is a great way to start off. And you never know when this friend or relative may have advice as to how to fix your problem.

Asking for help is another difficult step. You may feel humiliated, or like you have failed. But remember that you are not the first, or the last, person to ever have financial difficulties. Give yourself a break, beating yourself up will not help the situation. Just make sure that you learn from your mistakes.

You could always ask help from a professional money adviser. They should have experience and knowledge to deal with most problems. Get as much good advice as you can, from any source.

Be committed to take responsibility, and have realistic expectations for you can initial achieve when your commitment and enthusiasm is at its peak. Try and take away the emotions of the situation and approach the whole thing rationally and with a level head. It may take some time to sort out, but the benefits of keeping to your emergency plan will outweigh the consequences of continuing to ignore a financial crisis.

# Living with a Budget

Creating a budget is one thing; sticking to it is another. Different families will have different expectations about staying within the budget guidelines. Some may only use it as a general guideline, a yard stick to measure where they think they ought to be. Some families may view their budget as absolute, the rules are not to be broken. Either way, a family budget is still a strategic way for you to protect your family's financial interests and planning for the future.

However, just because your budget starts to work, and you can see a positive result in the amount save, does not mean that it's time to throw it out. Don't sit back and relax, throw your energy into making it a better budget. Budgeting is an on-going process in self-improvement. And what's more you never know what could be around the corner that requires you to spend money on. Knowing that you have something saved to pay for these emergencies can make the budget worthwhile for many people. It shows them that this is working.

If you do suffer from a setback, it can be very discouraging. You may feel like you have taken 2 steps back for every 1 forward. Unfortunately, this is part of life, and having a proper budget in place will help you deal with bad situations. You are more in control to be able work through any crisis.

Be aware that prices may fluctuation throughout the year. For example, when the kids are off school you are likely to be using more energy, and spending more on day trips, or phone bill etc. If you can recognise one of these periods several weeks in advance, you can save a little extra from your pay to cover the kids' expensive habits!

# Accepting the Negative and Positive Changes

There are always going to be factors in our lives that are going to change and these factors are going to affect our finances. The key to not letting this disrupt your budget too much is to plan ahead for what could happen and how you are going to handle this. The following are a few examples of how life can change our well thought out budget:

- Job Losses/ Major income loss- The financial implications of you or your partner losing your job are huge. You will have to consider making major sacrifices, not just small cuts here and there. Have a look back through you budget; can you really afford that vacation? Can you really afford to buy XYZ at Christmas? What can you reduce to save money? Travel costs, food costs, clothes budget? You will need to reclassify what items on your budget to reflect the change in context. This will be a good idea anyway, so that you can redo your budget to fit the situation.

- Promotions/ Major income increases- These will have an effect on your budget too. The extra money should be saved or used to clear debt. Or go towards one of those big annual expenses. Be sensible and realistic with your money. Accept and be proud of the positives, but keep in mind that negatives do happen. You do not want to get this extra money each month to blow it on things that you really do not need. The key to any budget is knowing how to apply moderation in your life. There is no reason to live as though you make a million bucks a year when you do not. And even if you do make more a year, why not put this money towards something that is going to affect your future. For example, many people who come into a promotion often put more money back for their retirement.

# The Dreaded 'D' Word: Debt

Unfortunately, it is a subject that we have to approach. No matter how much you wish it away, it's there. And the longer you leave it the harder it will be to challenge it. Repaying your debt should be one of your main priorities. Debt exists, so let's have a look at what you can do about it.

Debt is a wide concept which covers lots of different things like mortgages, car loan, credit/retail cards or overdraft. In this next section we will look specifically at credit cards as they are an easy and tempting source of credit and the result of bad financial decision making.

Prevention is better than cure. So, don't use your credit cards, or over draft unless you have a very good reason. Those who are serious about controlling their debt and get a better handle on their finances will find that cutting up their existing cards is a great way to ensure that you are not spending anything. However, keep one card for an emergency and leave this at home. Never go to the store with a credit card in your wallet, as it can be easy to use this for anything that you want. Don't use credit to buy indulgences that you don't have the ready cash for. You would be far better off saving for XYZ indulgence and buying it outright. You will save money in the long run because you won't be paying interest or charges. Keep in mind that interest rates on credit cards are compounded daily and monthly for these cards. This means that the balance you have is going to have a daily interest rate, and after each billing cycle another interest rate is tacked to it. When dealing with interest rates that are over 12%, the person could potentially pay back thousands of dollars more due to the interest that is charged.

If you are already in debt, then credit cards should be used in an absolute emergency. And you should dictate now what constitutes an emergency. For example, an unexpected medical bill is an emergency, getting the latest cell phone on the market is not an emergency.

Some pointers to consider;

- Have a look at the interest rates and charges on your cards. Is there a way that you can consolidate your debt? You can consider a consolidation loan to handle all of your debt, which can allow you to have one monthly payment versus paying each individual credit card. However, you have to consider the impact this may have on your credit rating.

- Be careful for sharp rises in rates or charges after the initial 3 months period. Credit card companies often lure you in with great deals which will only be replace by exorbitant prices later on. And many times, the fine print on these great deals states that if the balance is not paid in full during these introductory months, a person can incur interest beginning from the first purchase. It really makes a person consider whether the card is really a great deal or not.

- Watch out for late charges, and the interest added if you go over your limit. If possible, stay well away from the limit, as this will also help to improve your credit rating. If you do have a late charge and this is the first time, you can possibly have this waived by the company. Yet this is only going to be something you can try once. Though it may be a long shot, it never hurts to ask as the worse thing the company can say is no.

- Do not use your credit card at ATMS! Cash advances normally come with incredibly high charges that are the last to be paid on a credit card, meaning these fees stack up month after month.

- Avoid store/retail cards as these have extremely high interest rates from the start, some as high as 30% or more, which means one small purchase can easily amount to hundreds of dollars within the course of a few months.

- If at all possible, pay off your credit cards every month. Or certainly make more than the minimum payment. Aim to pay off the higher interest rate cards firsts. If you have more than one loan- apply this same rule. By just making an extra twenty dollars on each payment per month, you could end up paying an extra total payment by the end of the year, saving you hundreds in interest charges within a short amount of time.

- After 6 months of on time payments, try to negotiate a lower rate with your creditors. Many creditors are going to be interested in talking with you about this if you have proven to be a reliable customer and one in which they do not want to lose. Remember that if you do this, be courteous to the person you are talking to and firm at the same time. The nicer you are, the more likely the representative is going to work with you on finding a good middle ground on your interest rate.

Ultimately, remember that there is no such thing as 'free money'. No matter how good the interest rate, no matter how good the perks, you will have to pay back that money, and then some. And possibly the best rule to follow is AVOID NEW DEBT. It may be best if you remove your list from the pre-screened offers to avoid the temptation of getting a new card. This can easily be done and if it will save you from getting into more debt, it is well worth your time to do this.

Debt management can be easily adapted into your family budget, and provide you with a firm reason to stay well within your budget. It can be painful to look closely at your debt, but it is well worth it. Those who look at their debt are going to get a better understanding of just where they are spending their money. There are two methods that a person can go about using in order to really find out what kind of debt they are looking at. The first is to compile all of your credit card bills together. You will want to note what your credit limit is and just how much of this you have utilized. The other method, which may be the better option is to have a credit report that shows how much you owe to all your creditors. This is always a great way to see how credit worthy you are, as well as allow you to ensure that there is nothing out there in your name that you may have not opened. There are many ways in which a person can get a free credit report in order to get the process of debt management underway.

If you want to understand where you debt is accrued then apply the methods that we have previously looked at. Get your credit card statement and note down all the things you have bought. Categorize them into necessities/ emergencies, cash, indulgences. When you have done that, take a look at the charges. Are they standard charges? Late fees? Cash fees?

Using this method you will then begin to get a handle as to why you are in debt, and start to know what you can do about it.

If you are weighed down totally by debt, perhaps you should seek the advice of a professional. A specialist financial adviser, or a debt counselor can help you and offer you advice about the best avenues to go down, or offer you a personal debt review. For those who find their debt is outweighing their income then the aid of a professional is the only route to go. Debt consultation or debt management services may be of interest. These types of services can combine your credit card debt into one lump sum, while lowering your interest rates to help the total you pay become a bit lower than normal. However, keep in mind that these types of services are going to charge you for using their services, and when you go on a debt management plan this does affect your credit and also cuts all of your credit from the card. Thus, you can no longer use these cards. The typical debt management length is around five years, and then another two or three years to get your credit rating higher in order to receive credit card offers again.

A separate issue is student loans. Paying back a student load should be one of the things that you have written into your family budget- like the mortgage of car loan. If you find that you still cannot afford your student loans, then you need to look into what options are available to you. There are those families who will qualify for deference if they do not have the sufficient income meant to cover these loans and the basic cost of living. However, interest is also accumulated during these periods in which a person is not paying. You may want to consider other options such as consolidating payments into one lump sum or seeking help from a professional who deals with student loan debt.

Encourage your kids to take part time jobs to help and to show that they are involved and affected by the family finances. When a person feels more involved with their finances, they are more likely to take this serious. Plus, for your kids this is setting a great example for them so they learn the valuable lesson that money does not grow on trees, and a person has to work for what they are getting.

# Family Budgeting and Children

How can you ensure that your children are not overly affected by your need to budget? It's a hard question as, obviously, most parents want their children to have a fun and enjoyable childhood. However, children come with big $$ signs attached. But there are means of saving money while spending time with your children.

Be on the lookout for free activities. You can find adverts for such in local newspapers or TV channels. Activities days, open air concerts, free zoos or museums are all good ideas. Parks with play areas are ideal. Going for picnics to the beach, lake, park, forest or mountains are all good ways of getting your children in the outdoors, getting exercise and saving money too. You're avoiding having to spend money on expensive entry fees, food at cafes or restaurants and having to buy a toy or souvenir at the end of the day. Plus, you get to spend more quality time together as a family, rather than being separated in a huge amusement park.

It is best to steer clear of places where you are likely to be nagged into spending money! Such as taking your children to an expensive theme park with vendors and games to play. If you must go to one of these places, consider taking the cash that you can spend instead of using a debt card, as it is easier to overspend when you are not using cash money that is in your wallet.

Maybe you could budget for one special annual outing or event you can do as a family. This could be a camping trip, visit a relative who lives far away, or a visit to a theme park. Yet, this is only an option when you know that you have the money to spend on this and that this is not going to affect your monthly budget. You do not want to go and do these things if you are not sure you have enough money to cover your mortgage or car payment the next month.

Whatever you decide to do with your kids, explain to them, and even involve them in the budgeting process. As we mentioned early, they may pick up good habits. Hopefully, they will understand why they can't have everything they want. Young kids and toddlers have great imaginations. For example, if you buy them a big brand new toy, they will be equally as happy playing in the huge cardboard box that it came in. It may be a lot harder on older kids, who see their friends with whatever expensive new thing that their friends have. It may be hard, but at least no one could accuse you of having spoiled your kids! And in the end, your kids are going to appreciate being taught just how they should handle finances and they will implement this into their own financial mindset.

## ... And Finally

None of us want to feel like we are permanently short of cash. We all have dreams about having a bigger house or car, or an exotic vacation, and so forth. Setting up a family budget is a way of keeping your feet on the ground while you aim for whatever you dream of. But it is mainly a way of getting you to view your financial situation in a practical and realistic way. Making sound financial decisions may not be as instantly gratifying as indulging in little luxuries, but it is a much better way to live than to frivolously waste money and be constantly hand to mouth. The need for instant gratification is a mind-set that we need to get out of. And it is a mind-set that can ruin your financial portfolio for the rest of your life.

What we should be aiming to do is to maximize our income to the best of its possibilities, with the future firmly in mind. This means paying off bills and debt timely, saving for a rainy day, spending on essentials and potentially investing. Family budgeting allows you to get a handle on what is what, and enable you to stay in control of your money.

Hopefully, throughout these pages you have found some advice which has helped you to start off your own budget. It may seem very overwhelming at first, but the task should get easier as you go along. As you are honest with yourself and disciplined, you have the potential to set up a successful budget.

# We Want Your Feedback on This Book!

Our main purpose is to make sure that our readers get value from the books we publish and that they have a good experience with all of our products. We are always working to improve our books and other products with every revision and update.

Every piece of feedback makes a difference in this process. And we would appreciate yours as well - whether it is good or bad.

**Please take one minute to let us know what you thought by following this link:**

http://checkmatemg.com/feedbackbudgeting

www.ingramcontent.com/pod-product-compliance
Lightning Source LLC
Chambersburg PA
CBHW070715180526
45167CB00004B/1490